ORGANIZING AND USING INFORMATION

Beth A. Pulver and Donald C. Adcock

Heinemann

www.heinemannlibrary.co.uk

Visit our website to find out more information about Heinemann Library books.

To order:

☎ Phone 44 (0) 1865 888066

📄 Send a fax to 44 (0) 1865 314091

💻 Visit the Raintree bookshop at www.heinemannlibrary.co.uk to browse our catalogue and order online.

Heinemann Library is an imprint of Capstone Global Library Limited, a company incorporated in England and Wales having its registered office at 7 Pilgrim Street, London, EC4V 6LB – Registered company number: 6695582

"Heinemann" is a registered trademark of Pearson Education Limited, under licence to Capstone Global Library Limited.

Edited by Andrew Farrow and Marta Segal Block
Designed by Richard Parker and Tinstar Design Ltd.
Picture research by Fiona Orbell and
     Elizabeth Alexander
Production: Alison Parsons

Originated by Chroma Graphics (Overseas) Pte. Ltd
Printed and bound in China by Leo Paper Group.

ISBN 978 0 431 90818 2 (hardback)
13 12 11 10 09
10 9 8 7 6 5 4 3 2 1

ISBN 978 0 431 90823 6 (paperback)
14 13 12 11 10
10 9 8 7 6 5 4 3 2 1

British Library Cataloguing in Publication Data
Pulver, Beth A.
   Organizing and Using information. - (Information literacy skills)
   028.7

A full catalogue record for this book is available from the British Library.

Acknowledgements
The author and publishers are grateful to the following for permission to reproduce copyright material: © Alamy/Chuck Pefley p. **43**; © Cobis/ Image Source p. **34**; © Creatas p. **35**; © Getty Images pp. /Adam Gault **21**, /David Silverman **25**, /Keith Brofsky **36**, /Lenora Gim **4**, /Paul Thomas **40**; © iStockphoto pp. /Damir Karan **30**, /Mark Stout **7**; © PhotoDisc/Photolink/S. Meltzer **26**.

Background features and cover photograph reproduced with permission of © iStockphoto.

Every effort has been made to contact copyright holders of any material reproduced in this book. Any omissions will be rectified in subsequent printings if notice is given to the publishers.

Loughborough
COLLEGE est 1909

Contents

Some words are shown in bold, **like this.** You can find the definitions for these words in the glossary.

Getting Organized

You receive information every day. If you went to school today, you had several classes and learned hundreds of pieces of information. If you read a book, watched TV, or surfed the Internet you received information. If you talked to your parents or friends, you got even more information. The question is, what do you do with all this information?

When you are trying to answer a specific question or write an essay, you need to find effective ways of organizing this information so that you can use it. The better organised you are when collecting information and taking notes, the easier it will be to use your information. Good organization of your information will help you to clearly express the answer to the question.

Being well organized makes it easier to find things, saves time, and makes it more likely that you will come up with the correct answer or solution to your question or problem.

Tips for being organized

- Give yourself plenty of time – being in a rush leads to being disorganized.
- Keep your materials in one place.
- Make sure you have a clean, uncluttered work surface.
- Keep careful notes of where you find information.
- Create an order or a system that makes sense for you – not all systems will work for everyone.
- Try to avoid distractions such as TV and surfing the Internet for unrelated information.
- Clear away your materials at the end of every work session.

As a researcher and writer, you are responsible for presenting or using your information in the correct way. Different types of information require different presentations. In this book we will look at some different strategies for organizing your information, as well as ways to use or present that information.

Asking a question

Sometimes the best way to start a research project is to ask a question. A question will help guide you in finding the information you need. Some people refer to this question as a research question or a problem statement.

For some questions you will just need a one-word or one-sentence answer. Complicated questions or pieces of work may require looking at many different magazines, books, or journals. You may want to use the Internet or other electronic sources, such as online **databases**, to find the information needed to answer your questions or provide solutions to your problems. The more complex the question or problem, the more sources you are likely to need to examine. Being well organized will make these more complicated questions easier to answer.

Using graphic organizers

Graphic organizers are tools to help you organize your facts, so that you can communicate with your audience. Graphic organizers can be used in all subject areas that you study at school. They can also be used outside school to help you organize information to make decisions or solve problems.

Sometimes, before you begin doing research, you need a way to organize the information. A **KWL** chart can be very helpful in all stages of your research. K stands for <u>K</u>now, W stands for <u>W</u>ant to know, and L stands for what you <u>L</u>earn in your research. The first two columns are filled in before your research starts, and the last is filled in as you work. A KWL chart will help you sort out the facts you learned during the research process from those you already knew on the topic. It will also help you come to a conclusion when you fill in the "What I Learned" section of the chart.

Using a KWL chart will help you combine the information you already knew with the information you found and learned from. Using your facts will require that you use **critical thinking** or **problem solving** skills to answer your question or solve your problem. When you have worked out your answer or solution, you will need to communicate it to your audience.

A KWL chart

Topic: Reference materials

Question: How can I do research?

What I <u>K</u>now	What I <u>W</u>ant to know	What I <u>L</u>earned
Libraries have different types of reference materials.	Is the Internet trustworthy for research?	It is important to verify information in more than one source.
The Internet can be a good source of information	How can I tell if an author is reliable?	Sometimes books are quicker than the Internet.
		It is important to learn how to tell if an author is **biased**.

Different learning styles

Everyone has a different way in which they learn best. Some people learn best when listening to words, others learn best when reading words. Some people prefer to see things visually. Imagine you are trying to find out how to get to a friend's house. Do you prefer to be given directions, or would you rather look at a map? If you would rather look at a map, you may be a visual learner.

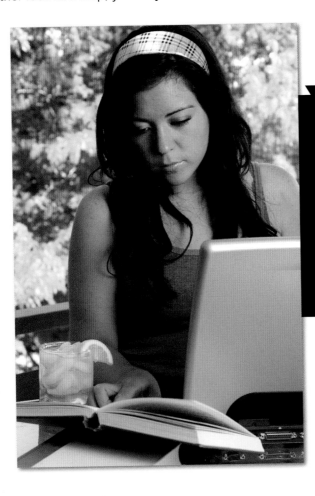

The first step to being able to use information properly is organizing it. A jumble of disorganized information can lead to errors.

Visual organizers

Visual organizers can be especially helpful for people who are visual learners. They organize written information in a **graphic** form. Visual organizers use geometric shapes such as circles, rectangles, or squares. Some popular forms of visual organizers are **concept webs**, **Venn diagrams**, timelines, **fishbone maps, flowcharts,** and story maps. Each of these graphic organizers helps the user to organize information. They are used in science, history, languages, arts, and maths. They are tools that you can use throughout your life to help you organize information and make decisions.

Venn diagrams

Venn diagrams were invented in 1881 by a mathematician called John Venn. They are especially useful for comparing and contrasting information. Below is the basic outline of a Venn diagram. Imagine you are studying household pets. You might label the left circle "cats" and the circle on the right "dogs." In each circle you would list unique aspects of each animal. In the middle you would list things the animals have in common, such as "mammals" or "come in several breeds." If you wanted to add a third animal, you would simply draw a third circle, making sure it overlaps with the first two circles at some point. The second example shows three pets and some of the attributes they have in common.

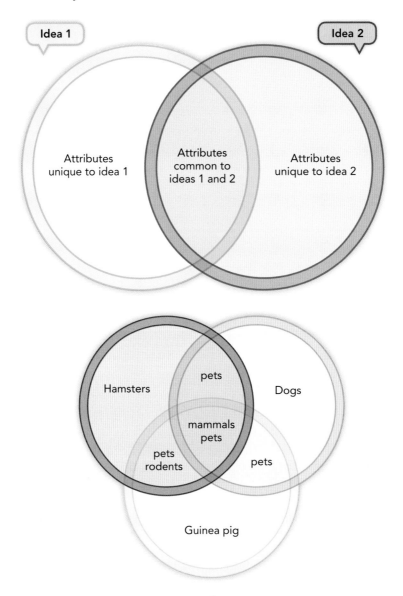

Timeline of the development of the Massachusetts Colony

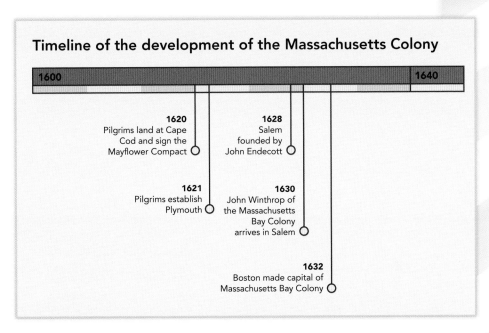

1600		1640

1620
Pilgrims land at Cape
Cod and sign the
Mayflower Compact

1628
Salem
founded by
John Endecott

1621
Pilgrims establish
Plymouth

1630
John Winthrop of
the Massachusetts
Bay Colony
arrives in Salem

1632
Boston made capital of
Massachusetts Bay Colony

Timeline of the development of the Virginia Colony

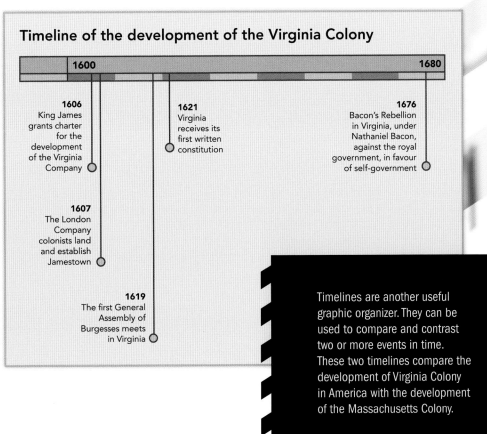

1600		1680

1606
King James
grants charter
for the
development
of the Virginia
Company

1621
Virginia
receives its
first written
constitution

1676
Bacon's Rebellion
in Virginia, under
Nathaniel Bacon,
against the royal
government, in favour
of self-government

1607
The London
Company
colonists land
and establish
Jamestown

1619
The first General
Assembly of
Burgesses meets
in Virginia

Timelines are another useful
graphic organizer. They can be
used to compare and contrast
two or more events in time.
These two timelines compare the
development of Virginia Colony
in America with the development
of the Massachusetts Colony.

Fishbone maps

A fishbone map, also known as a fishbone diagram or herringbone map, can be useful in organising information. These diagrams are especially useful if your research topic has many different elements to it. To fill in the fishbone, place the main idea in the middle. Each bone, or line, will contain a major point about the main idea. Then fill in the smaller sections with facts about those points.

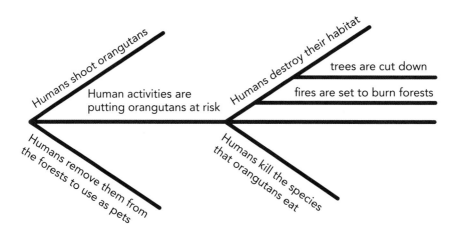

Using a concept web

When using a concept web, the centre circle contains your research question. Each main branch will become your main idea. Each main idea branch will have other branches, or subheadings. These subheading bubbles will be your branches, with bubbles containing supporting facts or details. These facts may come from your KWL chart. You will include the facts you already knew on the subject from column one, and the facts you learned during the research process from the third column.

Imagine a class of Year 9 pupils studying the endangered species of Central America. They are given a list of animals and plants to select from. One pupil selects the elfin tree fern, an endangered plant found in several Central American countries. This is a topic the pupil only knows a little about, so she doesn't have many facts in the first column of her KWL chart. She finds out many facts about this plant during her research. She finds out about the elfin tree fern's habitat, and why it is on the endangered species list. By organizing the facts in the concept web, the student is now ready to write an answer to the question "Why is the elfin tree fern on the endangered species list?" The facts already known are mixed in with the facts learned during the research process. Below is an example of the concept map for the research question "Why is the elfin tree fern an endangered species in Central America?"

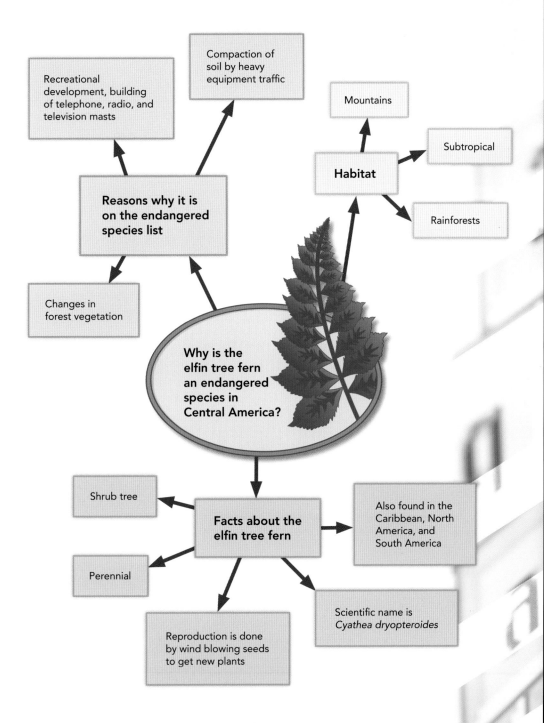

Recreational development, building of telephone, radio, and television masts

Compaction of soil by heavy equipment traffic

Mountains

Subtropical

Habitat

Reasons why it is on the endangered species list

Rainforests

Changes in forest vegetation

Why is the elfin tree fern an endangered species in Central America?

Shrub tree

Facts about the elfin tree fern

Also found in the Caribbean, North America, and South America

Perennial

Scientific name is *Cyathea dryopteroides*

Reproduction is done by wind blowing seeds to get new plants

The problem-solving model

Like the concept web, the **problem-solving model** will help you to arrange your facts. By organizing the facts in the problem-solving model, you can give a solution to the problem and present that solution to your audience. In the "problem" box, you will state the problem. The "possible solution" boxes will be filled in with possible solutions based on the facts you found in your research. You will use the facts you already knew on the topic and those you found during the research process. The "possible result" boxes will be filled in across from each possible solution with a possible result or consequence. The conclusion box will be filled in by you drawing a conclusion from each of the possible solutions and their consequences. By drawing a conclusion, you will present your own explanation of the solution to the problem and any consequences.

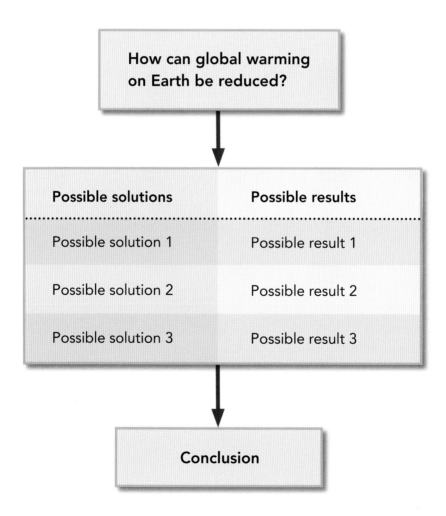

How can global warming on Earth be reduced?

Possible solutions	Possible results
Possible solution 1	Possible result 1
Possible solution 2	Possible result 2
Possible solution 3	Possible result 3

Conclusion

Using graphic outlines

We all have different ways of using information to answer questions or solve problems. If you are not a visual learner, you may not find graphic organizers easy to use. You may prefer to organize your information using a **graphic outline**. Graphic outlines are used to organize information, but instead of being a visual organization of your facts, it is an organized list arranged by topic and subtopic. Graphic outlines begin by stating the problem to be solved or the question to be answered. This would look like a title for the outline. Graphic outlines use a combination of **Roman numerals**, letters, and **Arabic numbers** to represent each topic, subtopic, and supporting details. The Roman numerals are used to indicate your main ideas.

What are Roman numerals?

Roman numerals are numerical symbols used by the ancient Romans.

Examples:

I = 1	VIII = 8	L = 50
II = 2	IX = 9	C = 100
IV = 4	X = 10	D = 500
V = 5	XX = 20	M = 1,000
VI = 6	XXI = 21	
VII = 7	XL = 40	

Using the example of the pupil researching elfin tree ferns, the main ideas are: facts about the elfin tree fern, its habitat, and reasons why it is on the endangered species list. Each main idea would be represented by Roman numerals I, II, and III. These are the same as the main idea bubbles in the concept web. The subheadings for each heading are represented by a capital, or upper-case, letter. Supporting facts and details are represented by the Arabic numbers 1 and 2 (see p.14).

Why is the elfin tree fern an endangered species in Central America?

I. The elfin tree fern grows in the subtropics of Central America.
    A. The elfin tree fern requires a subtropical habitat to grow.
        1. Rainforests create the moisture needed for the growth of the tree.
        2. The rainforests are high up in the mountains.

    B. The elfin tree fern is found in two countries of Central America.
        1. Costa Rica is between Nicaragua and Panama.
        2. Nicaragua is between the Caribbean Sea and the Pacific Ocean.

II. The elfin tree fern is a unique tree.
    A. The elfin tree fern belongs to the tree family and not the fern family.
        1. It is a shrub tree.
        2. It is a perennial.

    B. Reproduction of the elfin tree fern is done with seeds.
        1. Seeds are spread by wind blowing them to get new plants.
        2. The seeds must land on fertile soil.

    C. There are other facts about the elfin tree fern.
        1. Its scientific name is _Cyathea dryopteroides_.
        2. They are also found in the Caribbean, North America, and South America.

III. There are two reasons why the elfin tree fern is on the endangered species list.
    A. Humans have changed the environment that the tree grows in.
        1. They have built telephone, radio, and television masts in the mountains where the tree grows.
        2. There has been compaction of the soil by heavy equipment traffic where the towers were built.

    B. Other changes in the environment have endangered the trees.
        1. The forest vegetation has changed because of global warming.
        2. Global warming has caused changes in the climate.

This graphic outline uses complete sentences to arrange the topics, subtopics, and supporting details for the research question.

Key words and sentences

When you are developing your graphic outline, you combine the facts you already knew with the facts you learned during the research process. When using a graphic outline, every main idea, or Roman numeral, must have at least two subheadings or upper-case letters. Every subheading or upper-case letter must have at least two supporting facts or details. If you cannot fill these in, your main points may not be large enough to justify being main points.

There are two methods of using a graphic outline. One method uses complete sentences for each topic, subtopic, and supporting facts and details. The other method uses key words for each topic, subtopic, and supporting facts and details. The advantage of using the complete sentence method is that when it is time to write the rough draft of your presentation, most of the writing is already done. When using the complete sentence method, you must be careful to put the information down in your own words, and not copy from the source you are using. Advantages to using the key-word method are that it is easier to add in new facts, and you are more likely to use your own words when writing the draft copy of your presentation.

You may fill out a graphic outline, or any other visual organizer, and discover that your topic no longer seems to make sense. Perhaps the conclusions you thought were true at the beginning have changed. Perhaps there simply isn't as much information as you thought. This can be frustrating, but it is important to remember that these steps are all part of the research and writing process. This is another reason to not leave research and writing until the last minute. The process can take time and can have many false starts.

You may also find it easier to organize your thoughts if you are not trying to form complete sentences. Depending on how comfortable you are with your writing skills, trying to organize your thoughts and write your presentation at the same time may be difficult for you.

Taking Notes

Using note cards is a way to organize your information as you prepare your presentation for an audience. Examples of the type of presentation you could be making are a written essay, a computer-generated presentation, or a poster. Some presentations of your information may be done in the form of an oral report, or it may be a part of the presentation that goes with a poster.

Source cards

A helpful card to create is a source card. This card will be used when creating your **bibliography.** A bibliography is a list of the sources used in researching a topic. As you prepare your text, you will want to make sure that you give credit to the authors who provided you with your facts. If a fact was one you already knew before your research, you do not need to tell where the information came from. If you got the information from a source such as a book, magazine, newspaper, video, or website, you must provide information about that source. This is your bibliography. You may also use quotations within your essay or presentation as a way to give credit to the authors providing your facts. If you use quotes, you must still include that source in your bibliography.

Your source card should include the author and title of the source. It should also have the name of the publisher or producer, and the date of the publication or production. This information can usually be found on the **imprint page** of a book. Each source card should be labelled with an upper-case letter in the upper left-hand corner of the card.

Fact cards

After creating source cards, you will want to create fact cards. Each fact card should have only one fact on it. You should find a way to label each card with the source of the information. For example, label your first source card with the letter A. Then label each fact card from that source with a letter A. Another option would be to use different colours for each source.

Handyside, Christopher. <u>Jazz</u>.

Heinemann Library, 2006.

Jazz music began in New Orleans, Louisiana, as early as the 1890s.

Handyside, Christopher. <u>Jazz</u>.

Heinemann Library, 2006.

"Parker's playing style was more personal and expressive than that of other saxophonists. He seemed to be playing not out of a need to entertain, but purely to express himself."

Paraphrases and summaries

There are three types of information written on fact cards. They are **paraphrases**, **summaries**, and direct quotations. A paraphrase is the restatement in your own words of a fact found in one of your sources. A summary is a sentence that combines the information found in several sentences into one statement of fact. Direct quotations are statements taken directly from the source, without changing any of the words.

Direct quotations must begin and end with quotation marks to show that they are not your words, but those of the author. When using a direct quotation, it is very important that you make sure you have quoted the author correctly. Do not leave out any words or change words, even if the author has made a mistake. If you do, you could change the author's ideas.

Is it plagiarism?

Plagiarism is using someone else's ideas and information as if they are your own. If you take facts from a source, that could be plagiarism. It is acceptable to use information, facts, and even opinions found in other books. However, you must **cite** them in the bibliography, **footnotes**, or **endnotes** (see pages 38–39 for more information).

Plagiarism is not the use of common facts that everyone knows.

Fact taken from a source
At the mouth of the River Amazon, 4.2 million cubic feet of water empties into the ocean per second. (Taken from "How Great is the Amazon River," http://www.extremescience.com/AmazonRiver.htm)

Common known fact
The River Amazon in South America is the largest river in the world by volume.

Paraphrase

Paraphrases are restatements of information put into your own words.

Text:

"The Troubles are rooted in the split between the Protestant and Catholic communities, which can be traced back at least four hundred years."

Paraphrased text:

The split between Protestants and Catholics can be traced back four hundred years.

Summarize

A summary combines information into fewer words.

Text:

"Following an unsuccessful rebellion against British rule, Scottish Protestant settlers were deliberately moved to Ireland on the orders of the British king. They were "planted", or settled in Ulster, the region where the rebellion had been centred."

Summarized text:

The British king moved Scottish Protestant settlers to Ulster, a region of Ireland.

Text taken from *The Troubles in Northern Ireland* by Tony Allan, Heinemann Library, 2004.

You use direct quotations to provide support for the point of view being expressed in your presentation. You may also use direct quotations to provide context for your thoughts. Another reason to use a direct quotation is when the author has phrased something so well that you know you could not do a better job of it yourself.

It is important to keep careful track of what you are paraphrasing, summarizing, and quoting. You do not want to accidentally copy someone else's work and ideas without the proper citation or credit for them. That would be plagiarism.

Tips for taking good notes

- When taking notes, you will be looking at many sources of information. It is important to make sure that the information you are writing in your notes relates to the topic you will be writing about. You will want to refer back to your original research question, to make sure the information is related to your topic before writing it down on a note card.

- When you find a piece of information that you want to include on a note card, you must be sure to write the letter of the source from your source card. Then write the number of the page on which the piece of information occurs before you go on to the next card. If you do not do this, you will not be able to go back to the source to verify the information.

- All the information on the note cards should be written in the same place on the card.

- Source cards should have a letter in the upper left-hand corner and information such as the author, title, publisher, and date.

- Fact note cards should have the source letter in the upper left-hand corner, page numbers in the upper right-hand corner, and a single statement of fact per card.

- Once you have taken your notes, you must decide if you have enough relevant information to answer your question or solve your problem. You will take the fact note cards and sort them by topic and then subtopic, by referring back to your graphic organizer or graphic outline. This will help you to see where you might need more information. It will also help you to see which fact cards are not related to the question or problem to be solved. You can discard those fact note cards.

Working in a clean, comfortable space can help you organize your thoughts and your research.

Integrating new information

As you begin to prepare your presentation or write your essay, you will use your KWL chart to blend together the facts you already know with those you have learned from your research. You will do this by combining the information in column one of the chart, the facts you already know, with the facts in column three, the facts you learned. Using any of the graphic organizers – the concept web, Venn diagram, timeline, or graphic outline – will help you to put the information you have on your topic into categories. These categories are the headings and subheadings with supporting facts that add details to your essay or presentation.

Elfin tree fern categories

I. General information
   Scientific name, location, type of plant, life cycle

II. Information about its habitat

III. How the habitat has changed, why the tree is on the endangered species list

Once you have grouped similar facts together, you will need to prioritize the categories and decide which one your audience should know first. When sharing with your audience, you must have a beginning, middle, and end. The beginning should describe the question or problem to be solved. The middle of your presentation is the information you have gathered during your research. The end of the presentation, or conclusion, will describe the answer to the question or solution to the problem that your research supports.

Creating a rough draft

One way to decide if you have enough information is to begin writing a **rough draft** of your essay. As you write it, you will start to see where you need more information. Having an organized draft will make any gaps clearer. One of the best ways to organize your essay is to think about three parts: an introductory statement or **topic sentence**, supporting detail statements, and a conclusion. Whether you have just one paragraph or many, your piece of writing will probably follow the same format.

Graphic organizer for a paragraph

Main idea or topic sentence		
Supporting sentence or details	Supporting sentence or details	Supporting sentence or details
Concluding sentence		

For an essay with many paragraphs, you will have an introductory paragraph, several paragraphs of information that supports your introduction, and a concluding paragraph that summarizes the content of your essay. As you are completing your rough draft, you will know if you have enough information to answer your question or solve your problem. If you do not, you will need to research more information.

Graphic organizer for a multiple-paragraph essay

Main idea, introduction, and thesis paragraph		
Support proof details paragraph 1	Support proof details paragraph 2	Support proof details paragraph 3
Summary/concluding paragraph		

Applying Information

When you find information, you must evaluate it and decide if it is relevant to your project. Sometimes you will find information that does not agree with other information you have found on the topic. When you find conflicting facts, you need to verify which are correct by looking at additional sources.

When you find conflicting information, you need to consider its sources. Once you know these, you must decide if the author of the information is knowledgeable about the topic. You should also see if the information is up-to-date, by checking the age of the sources. Do your sources provide a list of sources used by the author? If they do, you can use these additional sources to confirm which fact is correct. If no list is provided, you must find new sources that confirm the facts found in your information. As you go through this process of working out the accuracy of the facts, you are using critical-thinking skills and problem-solving skills.

A critical thinker ...

- Gathers facts to answer a question on a topic or issue.
- Analyzes facts with an open mind for accuracy and clarity.
- Draws conclusions based on facts.
- Organizes information to answer questions.
- Is able to support their decisions with facts.

Critical-thinking skills

Critical thinking is the ability to analyze information and make decisions based on that information. You are thinking critically when you analyze the facts you have found with the information you already know. You evaluate all the information, and come up with an answer. You can give reasons to support your decision. Take for example a group of pupils asked to research the effectiveness of their city's systems for recycling waste. The pupils must adopt a position on whether or not the system is working as well as it could.

Before the pupils can decide this, they must research their city's recycling system. They will look at issues such as whether people are using it, how much it costs, and if it is environmentally correct. They will also look at the plans of other cities and towns, to see how they are different. When they have done this, they must organize their information and prepare their arguments to adopt a position.

A problem such as how to recycle materials is complicated and requires critical-thinking skills.

Conclusions

The pupils will demonstrate their critical-thinking skills by gathering facts, reading with common sense, organizing their information, and then deciding, based on the facts, whether or not their city's plan is effective. Their decision requires facts and careful consideration.

You will use the skill of critical thinking in every aspect of life, not just in the classroom. It is a skill used when making purchases, applying for university and jobs, and even when choosing friends.

Problem-solving skills

Problem solving is the ability to define a problem, identify and prioritize possible solutions and their consequences, select a solution, and then implement that solution to resolve the problem.

Take for example a group of pupils studying landfills. A landfill is a place that has been filled with household waste, which is then buried. There are many potential problems with landfills. The pupils must come up with some solutions to reduce the amount of waste going into landfills.

A landfill is a place where
waste is dumped and buried.

Define the problem

The pupils must first define or state the problem: "How can we send less waste to landfills?" After researching different types of waste and how they are disposed of, the pupils will decide on two or three possible solutions and their consequences. In a third step, they will decide which solution is the best. They must be able to defend their decision, and will use their facts to do this.

Like critical-thinking skills, the skill of problem solving is one that you will use on a daily basis in your life. You use problem-solving skills every day. For example, these skills help you to learn how to solve conflicts with other people, how to mend your printer or mobile phone, and how to make time for both friends and homework.

A problem solver ...

- Defines the problem.
- States possible solutions.
- States possible positive or negative consequences for each solution.
- Decides on a solution for the problem.
- Defends that solution with facts.

Communicating Information

If you are very interested in your research project, you may feel that writing an essay is a waste of time. After all, you could be spending that time learning more. However, communicating your findings is an important part of research.

As you organize your information, you will need to decide the best format in which to present it. Sometimes your teacher will tell you what sort of presentation you will be doing, and sometimes you will choose for yourself. The type of information you have on your research topic may also determine your format.

Essays

When you are at school, the most common form of presentation is an essay. You have probably already done a variety of types of writing. You may have written stories, essays, and reviews. Each kind of writing has its own style and its own rules. As you progress at school and in life, you will learn other types of writing.

Types of writing

Type	Definition	Examples
Narrative	Tells a story, can be fiction or non-fiction	Story, novel, letter, explanation, personal story, news story
Expository	Gives information, based in fact	News story, instructions, report
Persuasive	Writing meant to convince someone of your point of view	Request, book review
Scientific/Technical	Goal is to explain research or experimental findings	Medical report, research essay

Some essays or papers combine different types of writing.

Writing techniques

Depending on the goal of your writing, you will use different types of writing and different techniques. For example, imagine your goal is to persuade people in your city to recycle more. You will be writing a persuasive essay. You will be using facts, but you will be using them in a persuasive way. If you were writing an essay on how effective the recycling system is in your city, you would use less descriptive language. Below is an example of how the same topic might look in different types of writing. Some of the information given is the same, but the style is very different. To be an effective communicator, you have to know which style is best for your subject and purpose. Here are some examples:

Persuasive: "Imagine garbage seeping out of the landfill and into your drinking water."

Expository: "Nine out of ten people do not recycle."

Narrative: "When the council first announced the new recycling system, people were excited. However, today only one in ten people bothers to put plastic water bottles in a recycling bin."

How good is your writing?

- Is it clear and easy to read?
- Is it free of spelling and punctuation mistakes?
- Is it written in an appropriate form and style?
- Is it well organized and logical?

The easiest way to improve your writing is to read and write. When you read well-written materials, you learn the rules of writing without even trying. You see how writers use different kinds of words and styles for different reasons. Any kind of reading that you do can help you to see what does and does not work in writing.

Small-group presentations

Graphs, charts, leaflets, **flip books**, and essays are best used for small groups, where they can be passed around the audience. They can also be used as part of a larger display, where the audience can view them after the presentation. These types of presentation should have enough information included on the topic that they are able to stand by themselves, without an additional **oral** presentation. This means that you, as the writer, do not need to be there to explain the information in them. Many different topics can be presented in graphs, charts, leaflets, flip books, and essays.

Graphs and charts

Graphs and charts are best used to present the **data** or **statistics** you have gathered to answer your question or solve your problem. They are also a great way to display factual support for the reasons you came to a certain conclusion. Graphs and charts are great visual ways to display facts. They may be presented by themselves, or included in larger presentations such as essays or computer-generated presentations. There are several computer programs that will help you generate these graphs and charts, for example Microsoft Excel, Lotus 1 2 3, Corel Quattro, Mariner Calc, and iWork Numbers for Macintosh. If you have statistics on a country or scientific data, your best format may be a graph or table.

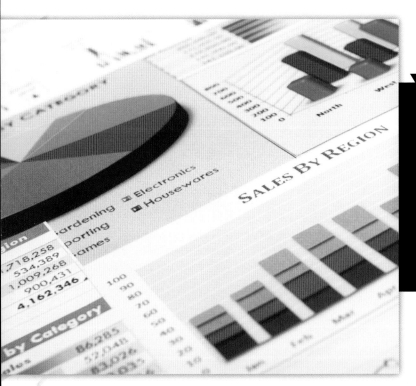

Graphs and charts can come in a wide range of formats, such as the bar graphs and pie chart shown here.

Presenting online

Writing for an online audience is different from other kinds of presentation, both written and spoken. Information that will only be read online must be well written. However, because people read from a computer screen in a different way from how they read a book, different rules and techniques apply. You are probably already familiar with some of these techniques from using e-mail and text messages. Although the formats may change with time, the methods you are learning today for organising and researching information will still be helpful.

Small-group presentation formats

- Graphs
- Charts
- Leaflets
- Flip books
- Essays

Leaflets

Leaflets can be single fold or bifold. A single-fold leaflet can be as simple as a piece of paper folded in half. A bifold leaflet has two folds dividing the paper into thirds. This will give you six areas in which to present information. The front panel is generally reserved for the cover, leaving the inside flap, three inside sections, and the back panel to present information.

When presenting information in a leaflet, you will use a combination of techniques. These techniques include the use of full paragraphs, bullet points, graphs, charts, and pictures or clip art in each section created by the folds of the paper. Leaflets can be generated by hand or on a computer. There are several computer programs that will help you generate these leaflets, for example Microsoft Word and Publisher, Corel WordPerfect, AppleWorks, and iWork Pages.

Flip books

Flip books are created by folding sheets of paper to create pages. The folds on each page are adjusted so that tabs are created when all the sheets are put together. Information is written on each spread of pages. The top page when all of the pages are folded closed is the cover. Flip books can be any number of pages or size, depending on the number of sheets of paper used and the size of the sheets.

Large-group presentations

When you have larger audiences, you will want to use formats that are easily seen from a distance. These would include posters, trifold display boards, and computer-generated presentations that are projected onto a screen. Many different topics can be presented in these formats. Results from science experiments are often displayed on posters or three-sided display boards.

Examples of large-group presentation formats

- Posters
- Trifold display boards
- Computer-generated slide show projected onto a screen

Oral presentations

There are two different types of oral presentation: formal and informal. Formal oral presentations are done when delivering an essay as as a speech, or when conducting a debate. Essays are often presented to your classmates in the form of a speech. For many of these presentations, you stand in front of your classmates and present your facts and the answer to your question or solution to your problem.

Debates

Debates are another way to present information. Debates require at least two peope, with each person taking a different a side on the question or problem. During a debate, the participants have the chance to express their views with supporting facts. After each participant has presented a position, the other participant has a chance to offer a rebuttal to that point of view. At the end of the debate, the participants each conclude or summarize their point of view.

Appropriate presentation formats for specific types of information

• Graph • Chart	→	• Data • Statistics
• Posters • Trifold display boards	→	• Bullet points of facts • Graphs • Charts • Pictures
• Leaflet • Flip book	→	• Bullet points of facts • Graphs • Charts • Pictures
• Essay	→	• Paragraphs of facts
• Computer-generated slide show	→	• Bullet points of facts • Graphs • Charts • Pictures

Both speeches and debates are usually written in the form of a paper or essay. For the actual presentation, the participants may have cards with notes from their paper or essay to use during the speech or debate. They may also have visual aides such as posters, graphs, charts, pictures, or leaflets.

Formal presentations

Formal oral presentations may be done using computer-generated presentation software. There are several computer programs to help you generate slide presentations, for example Microsoft PowerPoint, Corel Presentations, Lotus Freelance Graphics, and iWork Keynote.

When using presentation software, your slides should not have complete sentences or paragraphs. The information included on each slide should be enough for your audience to follow your presentation, but not so much that they can read ahead.

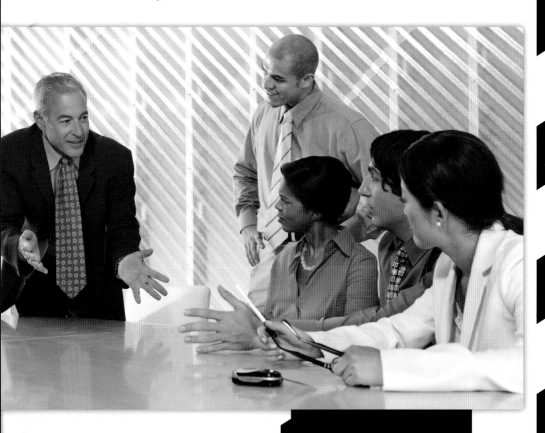

Debating skills will help you throughout your life.

Studying Insects

- What are insects?
- How can they be beneficial to the world around us?
- What can we do to reduce their harmful effects?

What role do beetles play?

When creating PowerPoint or other types of slide presentations be careful not to get carried away by inserting too many graphics.

The information should be presented as bullet points of facts, graphs, charts, and pictures or clip art, to enhance the presentation of your answer to your question or solution to the problem. The slides are like the illustrations in a book. The illustrations enhance the story, but they don't tell the whole story. The slides should be visually appealing to your audience. The use of colour, sound, and movement within the slides should be kept to a minimum, so they don't distract from the information on the slides or from you as the presenter.

Recognizing and Avoiding Plagiarism

Plagiarism is a very serious form of cheating. It is the same as when you look at someone else's exam paper and copy their answers. Plagiarism is when you use someone else's ideas as your own. These ideas could be written words, data, photographs, artwork, music, choreography for a dance, songs, videos, and films. It also includes plans or architectural designs for a building, designs for a dress, shoes, and jewellery. The use of someone else's words in an oral presentation is also plagiarism if you do not quote the person or cite them as a source.

Plagiarism is like cheating in an exam. You would not use someone else's answers, so why would you steal someone else's work?

Consequences of plagiarism

Teachers are usually pretty good at spotting plagiarism. The most common method is simply to talk to other teachers and get ideas on where the work may have come from. There are other methods as well, including free software. Many schools have rules and punishments for pupils who cheat. The consequence of plagiarizing, even accidentally, can be failing a project or exam, being expelled from school, or losing your job. To avoid any question of plagiarism, it is best to take careful notes and always credit your sources. When in doubt as to whether or not you should credit a source, it is best to do so.

Accidental plagiarism

Plagiarism is not always done on purpose. You can avoid the chance of plagiarizing by not paraphrasing when you are taking notes during the research process. Only write down facts. Then when you create your own essay or presentation, you will be using your own words. If you do use someone else's thoughts in writing, you must put quotation marks around them to show that they are not your own. It is important to copy quotations carefully and record the pages they come from when taking notes, in order to credit, or cite, your source.

Fair use

Let's say that *Star Wars* is your favourite film. You are not allowed to make a recording of *Star Wars* and sell it to a friend. You are also not allowed to take the script, shoot a new version of the film, and try to release it as a new film. However, if you are writing a research paper on science-fiction films, you are allowed to quote small parts of it. If you are doing a presentation, you can show parts of the film as part of your presentation. This is known as fair use. If you have questions about whether or not something is considered fair use, discuss it with your librarian or teacher.

The Internet and file sharing may be changing some of the rules on fair use. Before posting any comments, writing, or images on a website, you must find out what the rules of the site are. With some websites, putting your writing online may mean you give the site permission to use that writing in any way they want. Read all the regulations and any sort of waivers carefully before posting your work online. When using something you have found online, it is always better to give too much credit rather than risk not giving enough.

Citations

Including a bibliography, footnotes (listed at the bottom of each page), and endnotes (listed at the end of a chapter, article, or book) are other ways to avoid plagiarism. The information you need in order to create a bibliography, footnote, or endnote is found on your source and fact note cards. It is important to make sure you list all the sources of your information. The note cards will be used to remind you which sources you have paraphrased and which you have quoted directly.

Note cards will also become the source of information for your bibliography. A bibliography, or list of works cited, is a list of sources used during your research. Each type of source has its own way to be cited, but all entries contain basic information such as the author, title, publisher, and date of publication. Some sources, such as encyclopedia and magazine articles and Web pages, need additional information for their bibliography entries. You must include any source used, whether written, oral, video, or audio, in your bibliography.

Examples of bibliographic entries

Book
Author last name, first name. Title of book. Publisher, date of publication.

Magazine/Newspaper
Author last name, first name. "Title of article." Title of magazine/newspaper. Date: Page number(s).

Encyclopedia
Article author last name, first name. "Title of article." Title of encyclopedia. Volume. Publisher, date of publication.

Website
Author last name, first name. "Title of article." Title of Web page. Copyright date or revision date. Publisher of Web page. Day month year you saw the site. Web address.

There are many different ways to create a bibliography. Talk to your teacher about which method you should use.

Marking a citation in the text of a paragraph

Footnotes and endnotes must be listed numerically and consecutively in your essay. Footnote numbers should be superscripted (raised). In your text, add a superscripted number immediately after the quote or reference cited with no space. Here are some examples:

"There are some topics where you may already know many facts because of your previous experiences.[1] You may be only slightly familiar with some topics, and therefore only have a few facts about the topic. **You will first decide what you already know about your subject.**[2] These facts will go in the first column of the KWL chart. You will then need to determine what information you still need to find out. **These questions will go in the second column of the chart.**[3]**"**

Footnote entries at bottom of page

[From a book]

[6] Sigmund Freud, Totem and Taboo (Random House, 1918), p.17.

[From an encyclopedia]

[8] Lawrence A. Presley, "DNA Fingerprinting," World Book Encyclopedia, 2000 ed.

[From an article from a newspaper or magazine]

[10] Michael Friscolanti, "Convicts 'Morally' Fit to Vote: Supreme Court Ruling," National Post [Toronto], 1 Nov. 2002: A4.

[From a Web page]

[19] Canada, Indian and Northern Affairs, "Aboriginal Peoples Survey: From APS I to APS II." Facts from Stats, Corporate Information Management Directorate, Issue No. 15, Mar. 2000, 15 Dec. 2004 <http://www.inac.gc.ca/nr/nwltr/sts/2000-03_e.html>

A Rough Draft

Before writing a rough draft of your presentation, you will compare your note cards with your graphic organizer or outline in order to finalize your graphic organizer or outline. You may decide that you need to add or discard topics or subtopics, based on the information you have gathered during your research. Once you have finalized your graphic organizer or outline and confirmed that you have enough relevant information, it is time to begin writing a rough draft of your presentation. A rough draft is the first time you try to put all your information down on paper. It is for your use only. However, it is a good idea to keep a copy of it to refer to later.

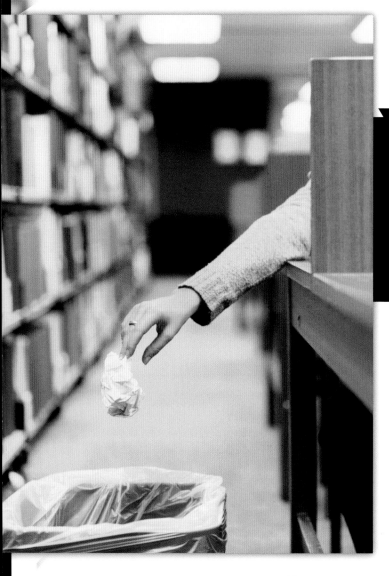

Writing a rough draft can be frustrating, but it is necessary to create a good presentation or essay.

Editing

Once you have completed your rough draft, you need to edit it. You begin this process by reading your draft and checking that what you have written relates back to the original research question or problem and follows your graphic organizer or outline. You will make corrections where you find mistakes or a need for more information. You should not be concerned about correct spellings and punctuation at this stage. Be sure to keep your note cards, because you may need to refer to them as you make changes.

Now it is time for you to share your draft with a classmate, parent, tutor, or teacher. The classmate will read it, checking that the introduction clearly states the question or problem to be solved, that there are enough supporting details, and that the conclusion clearly states your answer to the question or solution to the problem. Your classmate will make a note of any corrections or additions he or she thinks you should make. If you have been working on an essay for a long time, you may find it difficult to take suggestions from others. However, it is important to try to keep an open mind. A fresh set of eyes can help you see any mistakes and think of new ideas.

Once you have considered the corrections suggested by your classmate, you should correct any misspelled words and check that your punctuation is correct. It is helpful for someone like a parent to review your draft to check for problems as well. If you have been working on an essay for a long time, it can be hard to spot the mistakes.

Multiple drafts

At school, teachers may specify how many drafts they expect you to write. If they don't, it's up to you. There is no correct number of drafts. In general, you should make sure you leave enough time to write three or four drafts. As you gain more experience in researching and writing, you will learn how many drafts work best for you. The number may change depending on the type of project you are working on.

Summary

Every day you receive information. Before you can prepare a research project, you must learn how to organize the information you have found. You must also decide on the best way to present your information.

Graphic organizers and outlines

Graphic organizers are especially helpful for people who are visual learners. KWL charts can help you combine what you already know about a topic with the new information you learn during the research process. Other graphic organizers, such as concept webs, graphic outlines, and problem-solving organizers, can help you to organize your facts so that you can create a logical presentation. Concept webs are groups of bubbles arranged so that similar information is grouped together, but there is no order to them.

Graphic outlines also group similar information together, but they are structured so that the facts are in a logical order, making it easy to write paragraphs or essays. Graphic outlines use a numbering system that arranges your facts in a logical order. Problem-solving organizers, such as concept webs, help you to arrange your facts in bubbles, but the bubbles follow an order like the graphic outline.

Critical-thinking skills and problem solving

Some of your research questions or problems will require you to use critical-thinking and problem-solving skills. When you use critical-thinking skills, you are using your facts to draw conclusions and make inferences. Critical thinkers look at information with clarity, accuracy, and common sense, and make assumptions based on the information. Once your assumptions have been made, you will be able to answer your research question and communicate that answer to your audience. You will use critical-thinking and problem-solving skills on a daily basis during your life.

Oral presentations

Some presentations may be given orally. These might take the form of a speech or a debate. In order to give a successful oral presentation, you should first prepare it as an essay. Oral presentations may include any of the small-group formats to be used as visual support for the facts in your presentation or as handouts. Oral presentations may also be computer generated using a software program.

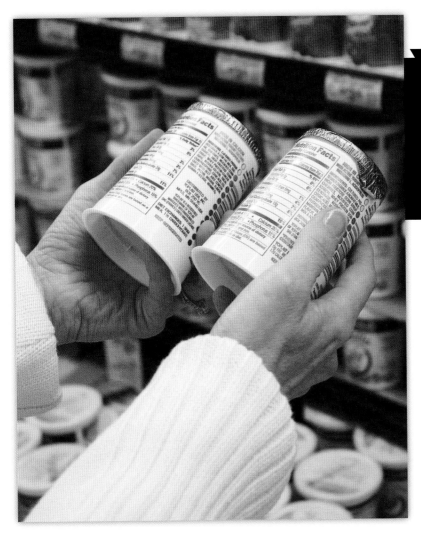

Plagiarism

Plagiarism is a serious offence. When you plagiarize you present someone else's words or thoughts as your own. Plagiarism is a form of cheating, even if it is done accidentally. You are allowed to copy small portions of an author's text or use an artist's image, song, or video as part of your paper or oral presentation. This is called fair use. If you are unsure of what is allowed and not allowed, you should ask your librarian or teacher.

When you first start preparing a report or presentation, all the information can seem overwhelming. Knowing some techniques for organizing and using information can help to make the process run more smoothly.

Glossary

Arabic number   most common symbol used to represent a number. Examples of Arabic numbers are 1, 10, 100.

biased   prejudiced, or with an inclination towards a particular point of view

bibliography   list citing each source used in researching a topic

cite   give credit to a work or author

concept web   diagram that shows the relationships between ideas. Concept webs are also sometimes called graphic organizers.

critical thinking   process of finding, evaluating, analyzing, and using information gathered from more than one source in order to solve a problem

data   collection of information

database   searchable collection of information that is stored electronically

endnote   note placed with others in a list at the end of a piece of work that gives the source of a quote or paraphrase of information used in writing the work

fishbone map   diagram that shows the details of a main idea

flip book   small book consisting of a series of sheets of paper folded to create pages of different widths or lengths

flowchart   diagram that shows a step-by-step progression using connecting lines

footnote   note placed at the bottom of the page of a piece of writing that gives the source of a quote or paraphrase of information found on that page

graph   visual comparison of similar information about two or more objects

graphic   presented visually

graphic organizer   diagram that shows the relationships between ideas

graphic outline   method of organising information using a combination of numbers and letters to indicate the main topics, as well as the subtopics under each main point

imprint page page at the front of a book that lists the publishing information

KWL chart table that helps to show what someone **K**nows about a topic, what they **W**ant to know about it, and what they **L**earn about it

oral spoken

paraphrase restatement of a fact from a resource that is put into one's own words

plagiarism claiming someone else's words or thoughts as your own

problem solving ability to define a problem, identify and prioritize possible solutions and their consequences, and then select a solution to solve that problem

problem-solving model diagram that states a problem, identifies and prioritizes possible solutions and their consequences, and then shows the solution to that problem

Roman numeral method used in ancient Rome to represent numbers by using letters of the alphabet. For example, I is the symbol for 1, X is the symbol for 10, and C is the symbol for 100.

rough draft first attempt at a piece of writing, usually improved upon and discarded

statistics collection of information or data

summary shortened version of information

topic sentence sentence that states the main point of a paragraph

Venn diagram graphic organizer that uses circles or squares that cross each other to show the areas that two or more things have in common, and the areas where they differ

visual organizer diagram that uses geometric shapes, such as circles, rectangles, or squares. These shapes, with information in them, are connected by lines that group similar information together.

Find Out More

Books

Critical Thinking Skills, Stella Cottrell (Palgrave Macmillan, 2005)

The Study Skills Handbook, Stella Cottrell (Palgrave Macmillan, 2005)

How To Write Better Essays, Bryan Greetham (Palgrave Macmillan, 2005)

Writing Winning Reports and Essays, Paul B. Janeczko (Scholastic Reference, 2003)

Cite Them Right: The Essential Guide to Referencing and Plagiarism, Richard Pears and Graham Shields (Pear Tree Books, 2005)

Websites

www.bized.co.uk/reference/studyskills/index.htm

This website is packed with information on study skills, covering many of the topics in this book and much more.

www.bbc.co.uk/schools/studentlife/revisionandskills

This part of the BBC website has helpful advice on how best to carry out research, improve your critical thinking skills, put together a class presentation, and structure an essay.

www.graphic.org
This site gives several examples of graphic organizers and discusses how they are useful.

Disclaimer
All the Internet addresses (URLs) given in this book were valid at the time of going to press. However, due to the dynamic nature of the Internet, some addresses may have changed, or sites may have changed or ceased to exist since publication. While the author and publishers regret any inconvenience this may cause readers, no responsibility for any such changes can be accepted by either the author or the publishers. It is recommended that adults supervise pupils on the Internet.

Further Research

Fair use and file sharing

Look at the information on fair use and file sharing on page 37. Find examples of websites that take contributions or photos from readers. Can you find any information explaining who owns the rights to the information posted online?

Venn diagrams

Look at the section on Venn diagrams on page 8. Who was John Venn, and why did he invent this diagram? What is the largest Venn diagram you can find?

Debates

Look at the section on debates on page 32. What are some famous debates in history? How have debates influenced political contests? What are some of the rules used in debates?

Waste and recycling

Look at pages 24–27. What is your town's recycling policy? Is the system effective? Where does the rubbish that you throw away end up?

Index